The funny family adventures of Hi and Lois continue in this *giant size* book filled with hilarious cartoons.

HI AND LOIS

Family Ties

by

Mort Walker and Dik Browne

tempo
books

GROSSET & DUNLAP
A Filmways Company
Publishers • New York

HI AND LOIS — FAMILY TIES
Copyright © 1977, 1978, 1979 King Features Syndicate, Inc
All Rights Reserved
ISBN: 0-448-16973-8
An Ace Tempo Books Original
Tempo Books is registered in the U.S. Patent Office
Published simultaneously in Canada
Printed in the United States of America

DIK BROWNE 7-28

THIRSTY, DO YOU REMEMBER THE DAYS BEFORE WE LIVED NEXT DOOR TO EACH OTHER?

SURE

10-6
DIK BROWNE

DO YOU THINK YOU COULD SWING IT AGAIN?

DITTO, HOW MANY PIECES OF BUBBLE GUM DO YOU HAVE IN YOUR MOUTH?

JUST ONE

7-30
DIK BROWNE

ONE?!!

YEAH... THE OTHER FOURTEEN PIECES ARE REGULAR GUM

8-6 DIK BROWNE

THE BOOK SAID SHIFT YOUR WEIGHT AND UNCOCK YOUR WRISTS SIMULTANEOUSLY.

TRYING TO DO THINGS SIMULTANEOUSLY ALWAYS THROWS MY TIMING OFF.

6-11

DIK BROWNE
7-8

WHEEEEEE!

THE GOOD PARTS NEVER LAST VERY LONG.